Epigraph

"The world teaches people how to work for money.
Very few ever learn the silent rules that make money work for them."
– Allan Mirembe

The Silent Rules Of Wealth

Allan Mirembe

Published by Kai publishing Co, 2026.

THE SILENT RULES OF WEALTH

First edition. March 26, 2026.

Written by Allan Mirembe.

Table of Contents

Introduction

Most people spend their entire lives chasing money. They wake up early, work long hours, and sacrifice their time hoping that one day they will finally feel financially secure. Yet despite all the effort, many remain trapped in the same cycle working harder every year but never truly building wealth.

Why?

Because the world teaches people how to earn money, but rarely teaches them how money actually works. From a young age, we are told to study hard, find a good job, and work faithfully for decades. But very few people ever question the system itself. Very few stop to ask why some individuals rise from nothing to build powerful empires, while others struggle their entire lives just to stay afloat.

The difference is not luck. It is not where you were born. And it is certainly not intelligence alone.

The difference lies in understanding the silent rules of wealth the unwritten principles that govern money, power, and opportunity.

These rules are rarely taught in schools. They are not usually explained in traditional education systems. Instead, they are learned through experience, observation, failure, discipline, and sometimes faith.

Throughout history, individuals who understood these rules changed their destinies. They turned small opportunities into industries. They transformed ideas into fortunes. And most importantly, they understood that wealth is not simply about money, it is about mindset, ownership, and long-term vision.

Money itself is not the ultimate goal. Money is a tool. It is a resource that allows individuals to create freedom, build influence, protect their families, and leave behind a legacy that outlives them.

But without the right mindset, money can easily disappear as quickly as it arrives.

This book was written to reveal the principles that many people discover too late in life. The silent rules that separate those who simply work for income from those who build lasting wealth.

Inside these pages, you will not find empty promises or quick-rich schemes. Instead, you will explore ideas about financial discipline, opportunity, ownership, faith, and the psychology behind wealth creation.

You will learn why some people remain trapped in a scarcity mindset while others see possibilities everywhere. You will understand why building wealth requires patience, strategic thinking, and sometimes the courage to step outside the path that society expects you to follow.

But perhaps the most important lesson is this:

True wealth is not only measured by the numbers in a bank account. It is measured by freedom, discipline, purpose, and the ability to shape your own future.

The silent rules of wealth are not reserved for a special group of people. They are available to anyone willing to think differently, act with discipline, and believe that their future can be greater than their present.

This journey begins with a simple realization: The rules of money were never hidden. Most people were simply never taught where to look.

Welcome to The Silent Rules of Wealth.

Rule #1

The Lie We Are Told About Money

From the moment we are old enough to understand the world, a story about money is quietly planted in our minds.

It sounds simple. Almost harmless. Work hard, get a good education, find a stable job, save what you can, and retire one day.

For generations, this formula has been repeated like sacred advice passed from parents to children, teachers to students, and society to the young. It has shaped the way millions of people think about money, success, and security.

And yet, something about this formula does not add up.

If working hard alone created wealth, then the hardest working people in the world would be the richest. The farmers who wake before sunrise, the construction workers who spend long days under the heat of the sun, the nurses who stand on their feet for twelve hours at a time, these would be the individuals building financial empires.

But reality tells a different story.

Many of the people who work the hardest often struggle the most financially, while others who seem to work far fewer hours accumulate incredible wealth.

Why?

Because the biggest lie about money is not that hard work is useless. Hard work matters. Discipline matters. Effort matters.

But hard work alone is not the system that creates wealth. What creates wealth is ownership, leverage, and understanding how money flows in the world.

The problem is that most people are trained to become workers inside someone else's system, not creators of their own.

Schools teach students how to follow instructions, complete assignments, and meet deadlines. These are valuable skills, but they are primarily designed to prepare people for employment.

Very rarely few traditional education systems teach students how to build companies, invest intelligently, or understand the psychology of wealth creation.

This is not necessarily because the system is evil. It is simply because the system was designed in a different era, when stability and long-term employment were the dominant paths to survival.

But the world has changed.

Today, information travels instantly. Industries rise and fall within years. New technologies reshape entire economies. Opportunities appear in places previous generations could never have imagined.

Yet despite this transformation, millions of people are still operating under the same old belief: that financial security comes from simply working harder and longer.

This belief is powerful because it feels safe. It promises stability.

But stability without growth can quietly become a financial prison. True wealth rarely comes from trading hours for income alone. Hours are limited. Energy is limited. Time is limited.

Every human being has only twenty-four hours in a day. But wealth is created when individuals learn how to build systems that produce value even when they are not physically present.

A business that runs without constant supervision, an investment that grows over time, an idea that spreads to millions of people. These are the foundations of financial leverage, and leverage changes everything.

It allows a single decision to multiply its impact. It allows effort to expand beyond the limits of time. It transforms income from something temporary into something scalable.

Understanding this shift from labor to leverage is one of the most important financial awakenings a person can experience.

But before someone can embrace this mindset, they must first recognize the illusion they have been living under. The illusion that working harder inside someone else's structure will eventually produce financial freedom.

For a small percentage of people, it might. For the majority, it will not.

This realization can feel uncomfortable at first. After all, the beliefs we grow up with often feel deeply rooted in truth.

But questioning these beliefs is the first step toward financial awareness.

Throughout history, every major shift in human progress began with individuals who challenged the accepted rules of their time. They refused to accept limitations simply because everyone else believed in them.

The same principle applies to money. When you begin to question the traditional narrative about wealth, you start to see opportunities that others overlook.

You begin to recognize patterns in how money moves through industries and economies.

You start to understand that financial success is less about working endlessly and more about thinking strategically.

And perhaps most importantly, you begin to realize that wealth is not reserved for a special class of people, but It's built by individuals who learn the silent rules and apply them with patience, discipline, and vision.

Seeing the System for the First Time

Once a person begins to question the traditional story about money, something powerful starts to happen.

The world begins to look different. You start noticing patterns that were invisible before. You begin to see how money flows, how businesses operate, and how certain individuals position themselves at the center of opportunity.

It becomes clear that wealth is not only created by effort but it is created by strategy.

For example, imagine two individuals.

The first person works ten hours a day earning a fixed salary. Every hour they work produces a certain amount of income. When they stop working, the income stops as well.

The second person spends those same hours building something that can operate beyond their personal time, a business, a digital product, a system, or an investment. At first, the income might be small. It may even seem insignificant.

But over time, something interesting happens, the system begins to grow, customers multiply, Investments compound, Opportunities expand, and eventually the system begins producing value even when the creator is sleeping.

This is the difference between income that depends on effort and income that depends on systems.

Most people spend their lives strengthening the first model while wealth builders focus on the second.

This shift in thinking is uncomfortable at first because it challenges the habits most people have developed since childhood. Society rewards routine. It encourages stability. It celebrates predictable paths.

But the individuals who build financial empires often think differently. They ask questions others rarely consider.

Instead of asking, "How can I work harder?" they ask: "How can I create something that works for me?"

Instead of asking, "How do I earn more per hour?" they ask: "How do I multiply the value of one idea?"

Instead of chasing security, they begin chasing opportunity. Opportunity, however, requires awareness.

Many opportunities pass directly in front of people every day without being recognized. Not because they are invisible, but because the mind is not trained to see them.

Consider a simple example.

Two people can walk through the same street filled with businesses, shops, and activity.

One person simply sees buildings and customers while the other sees potential partnerships, market gaps, and new ideas waiting to be developed.

The environment is the same. The difference lies in perception.

Wealth builders train their minds to observe the world through the lens of opportunity. They look for problems that need solutions. They study what people value. They notice where demand exists but supply is limited.

Every successful business, every powerful brand, and every growing industry begins with someone noticing something others ignored.

But there is another layer to this truth, one that many people overlook.

Opportunity alone is not enough. Many individuals recognize opportunities but never act on them. Fear, doubt, and uncertainty create hesitation. They worry about failure. They worry about criticism. They worry about losing what little they already have.

These fears are natural. But the silent rule of wealth is that progress often belongs to those willing to act before they feel completely ready.

No empire in history was built without uncertainty. No great company began with absolute guarantees.

Every entrepreneur, investor, and creator eventually reaches a moment where they must choose between comfort and possibility.

The majority choose comfort. A small minority choose possibility. And over time, that decision changes everything.

But before we move deeper into the mechanics of wealth, before we explore ownership, leverage, investment, and empire building, there is one foundation that must be understood above all else.

Money itself is not the most powerful force in the world. The most powerful force is mindset.

Because the way a person thinks about money will determine every financial decision they make for the rest of their life.

The Mindset That Controls Money

Before money ever enters a person's hands, something else controls its future and that something is belief.

Every financial decision a person makes whether it is spending, saving, investing, or building a business, is influenced by what they believe about money.

Some people believe money is scarce. Others believe money is abundant. Some believe wealth belongs only to the lucky or the privileged. Others believe wealth can be built through discipline, patience, and vision.

These beliefs may seem small, but over time they shape entire lives.

A person who believes opportunities are rare will hesitate when they appear. A person who believes the world is filled with possibilities will move quickly when they recognize one.

This is why the silent rules of wealth begin not with money itself, but with how the mind understands money.

For many people, their relationship with money begins in childhood. They hear conversations about bills, debts, and financial stress. They see parents working tirelessly just to keep up with expenses.

Slowly, a hidden message forms in their mind: money is difficult to obtain, difficult to keep, and often connected to worry, and without realizing it, they carry this belief into adulthood.

Even when opportunities arise, their mind quietly resists them because deep down they have accepted a different story, that financial struggle is normal and unavoidable.

But wealth builders rewrite that story. They understand that while money requires effort and responsibility, it also rewards creativity, courage, and intelligent risk.

Instead of seeing money as something to fear, they see it as something to master, and mastery does not happen overnight. It develops through learning, observation, and experience.

At first, the lessons may be small. Learning how to control unnecessary spending. Learning the value of patience instead of impulsive decisions. Learning how to recognize the difference between something that creates value and something that simply consumes money.

These small lessons gradually reshape the way a person interacts with wealth and eventually, the mindset begins to shift.

Instead of asking, "Can I afford this?" the question becomes, "How can I create something that pays for this?"

Instead of worrying about financial limitations, the mind starts searching for solutions.

This change in thinking may appear subtle, but its effects are enormous. Because the moment a person begins thinking like a creator of wealth rather than a consumer of income, their entire relationship with money transforms.

They become more aware of how value is created in the world. They begin studying businesses, industries, and innovations with curiosity rather than distance.

They observe how ideas turn into products, how products turn into companies, and how companies turn into empires.

And with each observation, their understanding deepens.

But perhaps the most important realization is this:

Wealth is rarely built through a single decision. It is built through thousands of small decisions made consistently over time.

Choosing discipline over impulse. Choosing patience over quick rewards. Choosing long-term vision over short-term comfort.

These choices may not feel dramatic in the moment, but they compound over the years just like investments.

Small actions, repeated consistently, eventually create powerful outcomes.

This is one of the quiet truths that wealthy individuals understand. Success rarely arrives suddenly. It grows quietly, often unnoticed at first, until one day the results become impossible to ignore.

And it all begins with a single shift in thinking. The decision to stop accepting the story you were given about money... and start writing your own.

Because once that decision is made, a new path opens, one that leads not only to financial growth, but to something even more valuable and that's Freedom.

Rule #2

The Poverty Mindset Trap

Poverty does not always begin with an empty bank account. Sometimes, it begins with an idea.

An idea repeated so many times that people begin to accept it as truth. An idea that quietly shapes the way individuals see the world, their opportunities, and their future.

This idea is known as the poverty mindset. The poverty mindset is not simply about lacking money. It is about the way a person thinks when facing money, risk, opportunity, and growth.

Two people can start with the same amount of money, the same environment, and even the same opportunities, and yet their outcomes may be completely different.

One may remain trapped in financial struggle for years. The other may slowly build stability, opportunity, and eventually wealth.

The difference often lies in how each person thinks.

A poverty mindset focuses on limitations. It asks questions like:

- "What if I fail?"
- "What if I lose what little I have?"
- "What if this opportunity is too risky?"

These questions create hesitation. They cause people to remain in familiar situations even when better possibilities exist.

This does not mean caution is wrong. Careful thinking is important when dealing with money. But when fear becomes the dominant voice in decision-making, it quietly blocks growth.

Opportunities rarely arrive wrapped in certainty. They often appear disguised as challenges, risks, or ideas that seem uncertain at first. Those who are trapped in a poverty mindset rarely move toward them.

Instead, they move toward what feels safe even if that safety keeps them financially stuck and over time, this pattern becomes a cycle.

A person works hard, earns income, spends most of it on immediate needs and short-term comforts, and then waits for the next paycheck to repeat the process again.

Years pass. Opportunities pass. And without realizing it, the cycle becomes a lifetime.

But there is another mindset that operates differently. It is often called the growth mindset or the wealth mindset.

A wealth mindset does not ignore risk, but it approaches risk with curiosity instead of fear.

Instead of asking "What if I fail?", it asks: "What can I learn from this?"

Instead of focusing on what could be lost, it focuses on what could be created.

This mindset does not develop overnight. It is built through exposure to new ideas, experiences, and perspectives.

Many successful entrepreneurs, investors, and creators share a common trait: they are constantly learning.

They study industries. They observe patterns. They read, listen, and seek knowledge from people who have already walked the paths they wish to explore.

Over time, this learning expands their understanding of what is possible.

The poverty mindset shrinks possibilities. The wealth mindset expands them.

But there is another reason the poverty mindset is so powerful. It is often reinforced by the environment around us.

If a person grows up in a community where financial struggle is common, the idea of building wealth may seem distant or unrealistic. When everyone around you believes something is impossible, it becomes difficult to imagine another reality.

But history has shown again and again that individuals can break beyond the limits of their environment.

Every generation produces people who rise from difficult circumstances to create extraordinary outcomes.

They do not escape their environment through luck alone. They escape by thinking differently.

They refuse to accept that the circumstances they were born into must determine the limits of their future.

Instead, they treat their starting point as exactly that a starting point.

This mindset does not guarantee immediate success. There will still be setbacks. Mistakes will still happen. Some risks will not work out as planned.

But each experience becomes part of a larger journey of growth. And with every lesson learned, the individual becomes stronger, wiser, and more capable of recognizing opportunities the next time they appear.

Breaking free from the poverty mindset is one of the most important steps toward financial transformation.

Because once a person believes that change is possible, their actions begin to reflect that belief.

They become more willing to learn. More willing to try. More willing to build something greater than what they inherited.

And eventually, those actions begin to create results. But understanding mindset alone is not enough.

Even individuals who believe in growth can remain financially stuck if they misunderstand the first real rule of wealth creation.

The Invisible Chains of Comfort

One of the most powerful traps of the poverty mindset is not obvious. It does not look like failure. It does not even look like struggle. It often looks like comfort.

Comfort can be one of the most dangerous places for someone who wants to build wealth. Not because comfort itself is wrong, but because it can slowly remove the urgency to grow.

When people become comfortable with a certain level of income, a certain lifestyle, and a predictable routine, they often stop searching for greater opportunities.

The mind settles. The hunger fades. And progress quietly slows down.

This is why many people remain in the same financial position for years or even decades. Their lives are not necessarily bad, but they are also not expanding.

The routine becomes permanent. Wake up. Work. Earn. Spend. Rest. Repeat.

At first, this cycle feels stable. But stability without growth eventually turns into limitation.

Wealth builders understand something important: comfort should be enjoyed, but never worshiped.

Growth usually lives outside the boundaries of what feels familiar.

Learning a new skill can feel uncomfortable. Starting a business can feel uncertain. Making investments can feel risky.

Yet these are often the very paths that create long-term financial expansion.

Those who escape the poverty mindset learn to treat discomfort differently. Instead of running from it, they begin to see it as a signal that growth may be nearby.

This does not mean recklessly chasing every opportunity. Discipline and careful thinking remain essential.

But it means refusing to let fear of the unknown control every decision. Because if fear becomes the dominant guide in life, progress becomes impossible.

Another invisible chain of the poverty mindset is short-term thinking.

Many people focus almost entirely on immediate needs and short-term desires. This is understandable, especially for individuals who have experienced financial struggle.

When resources feel limited, the instinct is to use money quickly so as to solve today's problems or enjoy today's pleasures.

But wealth is rarely built through short-term thinking. It is built through long-term vision.

Every powerful investment, every successful company, and every lasting financial empire began with someone thinking years or even decades into the future.

Instead of asking, "What do I want right now?", wealth builders often ask: "What will matter five years from now?". This question changes the way money is used.

A short-term mindset spends money the moment it arrives. A long-term mindset begins directing money toward things that can grow over time like skills, assets, investments, and opportunities.

This shift is one of the most important transformations a person can make. Because once the mind begins thinking long-term, patience becomes easier, discipline becomes stronger, and financial decisions become more strategic.

However, there is one final element of the poverty mindset that quietly holds many people back. It is the belief that wealth belongs to someone else.

Some individuals look at successful entrepreneurs, investors, or creators and assume they are fundamentally different.

They assume those people were born with special advantages, special intelligence, or opportunities that ordinary individuals will never see.

This belief creates distance. It turns wealth into something mythical instead of something learnable.

But the truth is far simpler. The individuals who build wealth are not perfect, they make mistakes, they experience setbacks, and they face moments of doubt just like anyone else.

What separates them is not perfection, it is persistence, learning, and the willingness to keep moving forward even when the outcome is uncertain.

When someone understands this, a powerful realization begins to form: Wealth is not reserved for a chosen few. It is built by people who develop the right mindset, the right habits, and the right strategies over time.

Breaking the poverty mindset does not happen instantly. It happens gradually through awareness, education, and disciplined action.

Escaping the Trap

Escaping the poverty mindset does not happen through a single motivational speech or a sudden burst of inspiration. It happens through small changes in thinking and behavior that are repeated consistently over time.

The first step is awareness. A person cannot change a mindset they do not recognize. Once someone becomes aware of the patterns that keep them financially stuck, fear of risk, short-term thinking, and attachment to comfort. They begin to see those patterns more clearly in everyday decisions.

For example, a person may notice how often they spend money on temporary satisfaction instead of long-term value. They may realize how frequently they reject opportunities simply because they seem unfamiliar or uncertain.

This awareness creates the possibility for change.

The second step is intentional learning. The world of money is vast. It includes entrepreneurship, investing, innovation, leadership, negotiation, and strategy. Yet many people never explore these subjects deeply because they assume they are too complicated or reserved for experts.

But knowledge has never been more accessible than it is today. Books, conversations, mentorship, and observation all provide pathways to understanding how wealth is built. The more a person studies how successful individuals think and operate, the more their own mindset begins to shift.

Learning expands perspective. And perspective expands opportunity.

The third step is taking small but meaningful action. Many people wait for the perfect moment before acting. They believe they need the perfect plan, the perfect amount of money, or the perfect circumstances before they begin.

But perfection rarely arrives. Wealth builders understand that progress often begins with imperfect steps.

- A small investment.
- A side business.
- A new skill.
- A conversation that leads to opportunity.

These actions may seem insignificant at first, but they create momentum. Over time, momentum builds confidence, and confidence opens the door to larger opportunities.

Another important part of escaping the poverty mindset is developing discipline.

Discipline is the ability to do what must be done even when motivation fades. Motivation can be powerful, but it is temporary. Some days it appears strong, and other days it disappears completely.

Discipline, however, creates consistency. It is the habit of continuing to move forward even when progress feels slow.

Many of the greatest financial successes in history were not built through sudden breakthroughs. They were built through years of disciplined effort, saving, investing, learning, improving, and expanding.

The process may feel quiet and slow at first. But over time, the results become undeniable.

Finally, escaping the poverty mindset requires something deeper than strategy or discipline. It requires belief.

Not blind optimism, but a steady belief that growth is possible. That circumstances can change. That knowledge can be learned. That opportunities exist beyond what is currently visible.

This belief fuels persistence during difficult moments. It reminds a person why they started the journey in the first place.

And gradually, something remarkable begins to happen.

The same world that once felt full of limitations begins to reveal possibilities. Problems begin to look like opportunities waiting for solutions. Challenges begin to look like lessons waiting to be learned. And money itself begins to appear not as an enemy or a mystery, but as a system that can be understood and mastered.

When this shift happens, the poverty mindset loses its power. The invisible walls begin to disappear. And a new chapter of financial awareness begins.

But awareness alone is not enough to build wealth. To truly transform one's financial future, a person must understand the first structural rule that separates workers from wealth builders.

It is a principle that has shaped industries, corporations, and financial empires across the world. **"That principle is ownership".**

Rule #3

The Power Of Ownership

There is a simple truth about wealth that many people overlook: Those who own the system earn the most from it.

Throughout history, the individuals who built lasting financial power were rarely the ones who simply participated in the system. They were the ones who owned pieces of it.

Ownership is one of the most powerful concepts in the world of wealth creation, yet it is also one of the least understood.

Most people spend their lives selling their time. They exchange hours of work for income. The arrangement may be stable and respectable, but it has a limitation that cannot be ignored.

Time is finite. No matter how skilled or hardworking someone is, there are only so many hours in a day. When income is directly tied to time, financial growth eventually reaches a ceiling.

Ownership changes this equation. Instead of being paid only for hours worked, an owner earns from the value created by the system they control or participate in.

A business owner earns from the products or services their company provides. An investor earns from the growth of the assets they own. A creator earns from ideas that reach thousands or even millions of people.

In each case, income is no longer limited to personal time alone. This is why ownership sits at the center of nearly every financial empire.

When someone owns something valuable like a company, an investment, intellectual property, or a system that generates value, they create a source of income that can grow beyond their physical effort.

But ownership does not always begin with grand ideas or massive investments. In fact, many successful entrepreneurs start with something very small like a simple service, a modest online business, and a single product.

At the beginning, these ventures may produce only small amounts of income. But what makes them powerful is not the initial size, it is the potential to grow.

Growth is the hidden advantage of ownership. A worker may receive a raise after years of service, but the increase is usually limited.

An owner, however, can scale the value of what they have built. A company can expand to new customers. A product can reach new markets. An investment can multiply as industries grow.

The more valuable the system becomes, the more valuable the ownership becomes.

This principle explains why some individuals accumulate wealth at extraordinary speeds while others remain limited by the structure of traditional employment.

But ownership also carries responsibility. When someone owns something, they also carry the risks that come with it. Businesses can fail. Investments can decline. Markets can change.

This reality is one reason many people hesitate to pursue ownership. The idea of uncertainty can feel intimidating.

Yet within that uncertainty lies opportunity.

Every major business, brand, and industry leader once began as an uncertain idea. Someone had to take the first step before success became visible.

Ownership is not about eliminating risk. It is about learning how to manage it wisely.

Those who understand markets, study industries, and think strategically often place themselves in positions where the potential rewards outweigh the potential losses.

Over time, their experience grows. Their judgment improves. And their ability to recognize strong opportunities becomes sharper.

Another powerful advantage of ownership is that it encourages long-term thinking.

When a person owns something valuable, they begin to focus on sustainability and growth rather than short-term gain.

A business owner thinks about how to improve products, serve customers better, and expand into new markets. An investor studies how industries will evolve over the next five or ten years.

This long-term perspective is one of the key differences between those who build wealth and those who simply earn income.

Ownership forces the mind to think beyond today. And in doing so, it opens the door to possibilities that many people never see.

But ownership alone does not guarantee wealth. There are many individuals who start businesses or buy assets without fully understanding how to make them grow.

From Worker to Owner

The transition from worker to owner is one of the most important financial shifts a person can make. But it rarely happens instantly.

For most people, ownership begins as a second path, not the first. They may still work a job while slowly building something that belongs to them.

This might be a small business started during evenings or weekends. It might be a product they develop and sell. It might be money invested into assets that grow over time.

At first, these efforts may seem small compared to a regular paycheck. The income might be unpredictable. Progress might feel slow.

This stage often tests patience. Many people quit too early because the results do not appear quickly enough. They compare their small beginning to someone else's finished success and feel discouraged. But what they do not see is that every successful owner once started at the same point.

Every global company began with a small operation. Every powerful investment portfolio began with a first investment. Every successful entrepreneur once had doubts about whether their idea would work.

The early stage of ownership is not about instant wealth. It is about building the foundation. This foundation includes learning how markets work, understanding customers, managing money wisely, and improving decision-making over time.

Mistakes during this stage are almost unavoidable. A product may not sell as expected. A business idea may need adjustment. An investment may lose value before gaining it.

But each mistake carries lessons that strengthen the owner's understanding.

In fact, many experienced entrepreneurs say that their early failures were some of their most valuable teachers.

Failure reveals weaknesses in strategy. It forces individuals to adapt, improve, and become more resilient.

Those who continue learning eventually develop something powerful: "experience". And experience creates confidence. With confidence comes better decisions. Better decisions lead to stronger opportunities.

And over time, the systems they build begin to grow more stable and profitable.

Another important part of becoming an owner is learning to create value. Money flows toward value.

If a business solves a problem, customers are willing to pay for that solution. If an investment supports a growing industry, its value increases as demand rises.

Understanding value changes the way a person sees the world.

Instead of asking, "How can I make money?", the owner asks: "What problem can I solve?"

This question is powerful because the greatest fortunes in history were built by individuals who solved problems for large numbers of people.

Some improved communication. Others transformed transportation, technology, healthcare, or entertainment.

The scale of the solution determines the scale of the reward. However, not every valuable idea requires global reach.

A local business that serves its community well can become highly successful. A specialized service can generate consistent income. A niche product can build a loyal customer base.

Ownership is not about copying someone else's path. It is about recognizing opportunities that align with your skills, interests, and environment.

Over time, these opportunities begin to connect. One business may create the capital to invest in another. One investment may open doors to new partnerships. One idea may evolve into something far greater than originally imagined.

This is how financial ecosystems are built.

But as powerful as ownership is, it still has limits if it depends entirely on the owner's personal effort.

A business that cannot operate without its founder becomes another form of employment.

An investment that grows slowly without strategy may take decades to create significant wealth.

To truly unlock the power of ownership, something else must enter the equation.

A force that allows one person's effort to multiply beyond their individual capacity, and that force is **"leverage".**

Rule #4

The Force Called Leverage

Leverage is not only about money or business systems. In many cases, the greatest leverage comes from something far less visible: knowledge.

A person who learns a valuable skill once can use that skill repeatedly throughout their lifetime. A programmer who understands how to build software can create products used by thousands. A writer who learns how to communicate ideas clearly can influence readers across the world.

The effort required to learn the skill happens once. But the value created by that skill can continue for years. That is the quiet advantage of intellectual leverage.

The modern world has made this form of leverage more powerful than ever before. A single video can educate millions. A digital product can be downloaded across continents. A new idea shared online can spark conversations in places the creator has never even visited.

In previous generations, opportunities were often limited by geography. A person's influence was usually restricted to their town or local community.

Today, the internet has changed that equation.

A young entrepreneur with creativity and discipline can build a global audience from a small room with nothing more than a laptop and a reliable connection.

This transformation means that leverage is no longer reserved only for large corporations or wealthy investors. It is available to anyone willing to learn how to use the tools of the modern world.

But tools alone are not enough.

Without discipline and vision, even the greatest opportunities can be wasted.

For example

Consider the story of a young man who began selling simple handmade bracelets in a local market.

At first, his operation was small. He worked alone, producing only a few items each day. The income was modest, just enough to cover basic needs.

But instead of remaining at that level, he began thinking differently.

He realized that if he taught others how to make the same bracelets, production could increase. Soon he invited two friends to join him. Together they produced more items than he could alone.

Then he discovered online marketplaces.

Instead of selling only to people who passed by his market stall, he began offering his products online. Orders started arriving from customers in other cities.

Later, he reinvested part of his earnings into better tools and materials. The quality of the bracelets improved, and demand grew even further.

What began as a small personal effort gradually transformed into a growing business supported by a team and a digital platform.

That transformation happened because he discovered leverage.

He multiplied his effort through people, technology, and reinvestment.

The Leverage Trap

However, leverage can also become dangerous when used without wisdom.

Many people attempt to grow too quickly. They borrow large amounts of money, take on responsibilities they cannot manage, or expand businesses before strong foundations exist.

Instead of multiplying success, leverage begins multiplying risk.

This is why patience remains one of the most valuable traits in the journey toward wealth.

- Strong foundations must always come first.
- Systems must be stable.
- Income must be reliable.

Only then should leverage be expanded carefully and strategically.

Those who rush often discover that rapid growth without discipline can collapse just as quickly.

Learning to Multiply Value

One of the most powerful questions anyone can ask when building wealth is this: "How can I create value that continues working even when I am not?"

- A farmer plants seeds that continue growing long after they are placed in the soil.

- An author writes a book that continues reaching readers years later.

- An entrepreneur builds systems that generate revenue even when they are not physically present.

In each case, the individual has created something that outlives the initial effort.

That is the true power of leverage. It turns work into lasting value.

The silent rule

When people rely only on their personal labor, their financial growth remains limited by time and energy.

But when they begin using leverage—through knowledge, technology, people, and systems, their potential expands dramatically.

The fourth silent rule of wealth can therefore be understood in a simple statement:

- Effort creates opportunity. Leverage multiplies it.

Yet even with leverage, wealth cannot survive without a powerful habit that protects it.

Many individuals have earned fortunes only to lose them because they lacked **"discipline"**.

Rule #5

The Law Of Financial Discipline

If leverage helps wealth grow faster, discipline is what protects it.

Many people believe the hardest part of becoming wealthy is earning money. In reality, earning money is only the beginning. The true challenge is managing money wisely once it arrives.

History has shown countless examples of individuals who earned enormous incomes but still ended up with nothing. Professional athletes, celebrities, business owners, and lottery winners have all experienced this painful reality.

Money came quickly. But it also disappeared quickly.

Why?

Because wealth without discipline is like water poured into a broken container. No matter how much you add, it will eventually leak away.

Financial discipline is the habit of controlling money instead of allowing money to control you.

It requires patience, awareness, and the ability to delay immediate pleasure for greater long-term rewards.

A Lesson From Two Friends

Imagine two friends who begin working at the same company. Both receive similar salaries. Both have similar opportunities.

But over time, their financial lives begin to look very different.

The first friend spends most of his earnings as soon as they arrive. He buys the newest phone every year, expensive clothes, and takes frequent trips he cannot comfortably afford. Whenever extra money appears, it quickly disappears on things that bring temporary excitement.

The second friend chooses a different path. He still enjoys life, but he spends carefully. He sets aside a portion of his income every month. Some of that money goes into savings, while another portion goes toward small investments.

Years pass.

The first friend continues earning money, yet he constantly feels financially pressured. Unexpected expenses create stress because there is no safety net.

The second friend gradually builds stability. His savings grow, his investments begin generating returns, and he gains confidence knowing that his future is becoming more secure.

Both men earned similar incomes. But their habits created completely different outcomes. That is the quiet power of financial discipline.

The Temptation of Immediate Rewards

One of the greatest obstacles to discipline is the human desire for instant gratification.

People naturally enjoy rewards that arrive quickly. Buying something new provides immediate excitement. Spending money can create a temporary feeling of success.

But this excitement rarely lasts. Soon, another desire appears, and the cycle repeats.

The problem is that constant spending leaves little room for long-term growth.

Discipline requires the ability to pause and ask an important question before making financial decisions:

- "Is this helping my future, or only satisfying the present moment?"

This simple question can transform financial behavior over time.

The Power of Consistency

Financial discipline does not require extreme sacrifice. It requires consistency.

Saving a small portion of income every month may seem insignificant at first. But over time, those small actions accumulate.

A person who saves and invests regularly for ten years will often achieve far greater financial stability than someone who waits for a single large opportunity.

Consistency turns small actions into powerful results. It is similar to planting seeds.

At first, nothing appears to happen. But beneath the surface, growth is slowly taking place. Eventually, the results become visible. The same principle applies to money.

Learning to Live Below Your Means

Another important principle of financial discipline is learning to live below your means.

This idea does not mean living in constant restriction or avoiding enjoyment. Instead, it means ensuring that spending never exceeds what income can comfortably support.

Many individuals increase their lifestyle every time their income rises. When they earn more, they spend more. When they receive a promotion, they upgrade everything.

As a result, they remain financially fragile despite higher earnings. Those who practice discipline take a different approach.

When income increases, they allow their investments and savings to grow as well.

Instead of using every new dollar for lifestyle upgrades, they direct some of that money toward assets that will strengthen their future, and this creates a powerful advantage over time.

The Silent Rule

The fifth silent rule of wealth can be summarized in a simple truth:

- Making money is important. Keeping and managing money is essential.
- Without discipline, wealth is temporary. With discipline, wealth becomes sustainable.

But there is another powerful strategy that allows disciplined individuals to accelerate their financial progress even further.

Instead of relying on a single source of income, they create multiple paths for money to flow into their lives.

This approach not only increases earnings but also protects against unexpected setbacks.

Rule #6

Multiple Streams of Income

One of the most dangerous financial positions a person can have is depending entirely on a single source of income.

For many people, this source is their job. Every month they receive a paycheck, and that paycheck supports their entire lifestyle including rent, food, transportation, and everything else.

At first, this may seem normal. After all, most societies are built around the idea of working for a salary.

But the silent risk in this system is simple.

If that single source disappears, the entire financial structure collapses.

Jobs can be lost. Companies can close. Economic conditions can change without warning. When income depends on only one source, even a small disruption can create serious financial pressure.

This is why many financially successful individuals focus on building multiple streams of income, and instead of relying on one river of money, they create several.

The Power of Diversification

Imagine a farmer who depends on only one crop for survival. If the weather damages that crop, the farmer loses everything for the season.

But another farmer plants several different crops. If one harvest fails, the others can still provide income.

This idea is known as diversification, and it applies strongly to finance.

Multiple income streams create stability. When one stream slows down, others can continue flowing.

Over time, these streams can even grow large enough to support complete financial independence.

Types of Income Streams

Income can come from many different sources. Some require active effort, while others continue generating money with minimal daily involvement.

Here are a few common examples:

- **Earned Income**

This is the most familiar form of money, earned from employment or providing services.

- **Business Income**

Money generated from owning a business or selling products and services.

- **Investment Income**

Returns from assets such as stocks, bonds, or other financial investments.

- **Rental Income**

Money earned from property that others pay to use.

- **Royalty Income**

Income generated from intellectual property such as books, music, or digital products.

Each type of income plays a different role in the journey toward wealth. The key is gradually expanding beyond a single source.

Many successful entrepreneurs begin with a primary job or business and slowly add additional streams over time.

A Story of Gradual Growth

Consider the story of a young teacher who loved photography.

At first, photography was simply a hobby. On weekends, she enjoyed capturing images of nature and local events.

One day a friend asked her to photograph a small family celebration. She accepted the opportunity and earned a modest payment.

Encouraged by the experience, she began offering photography services occasionally on weekends.

Months later, she started sharing her photos online. Some of her images began attracting attention. Soon she was selling digital copies to people who admired her work.

Later still, she created an online course teaching beginners how to improve their photography skills.

What started as a simple hobby slowly transformed into several income streams:

- Weekend photography sessions.
- Online photo sales.
- Educational courses.

Her teaching job remained her primary income, but these additional streams provided financial flexibility and new opportunities.

Over time, her total earnings became far greater than what one job alone could provide.

Building Streams With Patience

Creating multiple income streams does not happen overnight. It often begins with small experiments. A side project, a skill developed during spare time, or a modest investment.

Some ideas succeed. Others fail. But each attempt teaches valuable lessons.

The goal is not immediate perfection. The goal is steady expansion.

Even one additional income stream can significantly strengthen financial stability. Two or three streams create even greater security.

And as experience grows, those streams can evolve into powerful sources of long-term wealth.

The Silent Rule

The sixth silent rule of wealth can be summarized clearly:

- Financial security grows stronger when income flows from many directions.

Those who rely on only one source remain vulnerable to sudden change. Those who build multiple streams create resilience. Their financial future becomes less fragile and far more flexible.

Yet even with several streams of income, there is another factor that determines whether wealth continues growing.

That factor is not money itself. It is the mindset that governs financial decisions.

Because the greatest battles with money often take place not in the marketplace, but in the human mind.

Rule #7

The Psychology of Wealth

Money is often discussed as if it were purely mathematical. People talk about numbers, investments, profits, and markets. While these elements are important, they represent only part of the picture.

Behind every financial decision is something far more powerful: the human mind.

The way a person thinks about money can shape their entire financial future. Two individuals with the same income, the same opportunities, and the same education can end up in completely different financial positions simply because their mindsets are different.

This is why understanding the psychology of wealth is essential.

Wealth is not only built through strategies and investments. It is built through beliefs, habits, and emotional discipline.

The Scarcity Mindset

Many people grow up with what psychologists call a scarcity mindset.

This mindset develops when individuals constantly feel that resources are limited and opportunities are rare. People with this perspective often believe that wealth is reserved only for a small group of fortunate individuals.

As a result, they may avoid taking risks, investing in themselves, or pursuing ambitious goals. Deep down, they believe success is unlikely.

This belief quietly influences their decisions. When opportunities appear, they hesitate. When challenges arise, they retreat.

Over time, this mindset becomes a barrier that prevents growth.

The Abundance Mindset

In contrast, individuals with an abundance mindset see the world differently.

They believe that opportunities exist everywhere and that value can always be created. Instead of focusing on limitations, they focus on possibilities.

This does not mean they ignore difficulties or pretend challenges do not exist. Rather, they approach obstacles with the belief that solutions can be found.

When setbacks occur, they ask:

- "What can I learn from this experience?"
- "How can I improve my strategy?"
- "How can this challenge make me stronger?"

This perspective allows them to continue moving forward even when circumstances are difficult.

A Story of Two Entrepreneurs

Consider two aspiring entrepreneurs who both start small businesses.

The first entrepreneur becomes discouraged when sales grow slowly. After a few months of limited progress, he concludes that the business will never succeed. He closes the venture and returns to searching for another idea.

The second entrepreneur faces the same slow beginning but reacts differently. Instead of giving up, she studies the problem. She improves her marketing, refines her product, and listens carefully to customer feedback.

Gradually, the business begins to improve. Months later, her persistence starts producing results.

Years later, the same business becomes a stable and profitable operation.

The difference between the two entrepreneurs was not intelligence or opportunity. It was mindset.

Emotional Control and Money

Another important aspect of financial psychology is emotional control.

Money decisions are often influenced by feelings such as fear, excitement, greed, or anxiety.

For example:

When markets rise quickly, some investors become overly confident and take unnecessary risks.

When markets decline, others panic and sell their investments at the worst possible moment.

In both cases, emotions override rational thinking.

Successful wealth builders learn to recognize these emotional impulses and maintain discipline despite them.

They make decisions based on long-term strategy rather than short-term feelings.

This ability to remain calm during uncertainty is one of the most valuable financial skills a person can develop.

Self-Belief and Opportunity

Perhaps the most powerful psychological factor in wealth creation is self-belief.

Many great achievements begin with an idea that others initially doubt.

If individuals abandon their vision simply because others question it, many innovations would never exist.

But those who believe strongly in their ability to learn, adapt, and grow often continue moving forward despite skepticism.

Their confidence allows them to take action while others hesitate. Over time, this action creates opportunities that would otherwise remain invisible.

The Silent Rule

The seventh silent rule of wealth is this:

- Your financial future is shaped not only by your actions, but by the way you think.

A disciplined mind makes better decisions. A resilient mindset overcomes setbacks. And a confident belief in growth allows individuals to pursue opportunities that others may never attempt.

But mindset alone is not enough.

To transform ideas into lasting success, individuals must also develop a clear direction for their lives.

They must know where they are going and why. This clarity becomes the foundation for powerful progress.

Rule #8

The Power of Vision

Every great achievement begins with something invisible.

Before businesses are built, before fortunes are created, before ideas change the world, there is always a vision.

Vision is the ability to see possibilities that do not yet exist. It is the quiet voice that says, "Something greater can be built here."

Without vision, people often move through life reacting to circumstances instead of shaping them. They follow paths created by others, working hard but never directing their effort toward a clear destination.

But individuals who possess strong vision approach life differently. They do not simply ask, "What is happening today?"

They ask a much more powerful question: "What kind of future do I want to create?"

This question changes everything.

Seeing Beyond the Present

Many of the most successful entrepreneurs and innovators began their journeys with nothing more than a strong belief in an idea.

When others saw limitations, they saw potential. When others focused on immediate obstacles, they focused on long-term possibilities.

Vision allows people to look beyond the present moment and imagine a different future.

A small shop owner may envision building a national brand.

A young writer may imagine creating books that inspire readers across the world.

A student with limited resources may dream of building a company that transforms an entire industry.

These visions may appear unrealistic at first. But history has repeatedly shown that progress often begins with ideas that once seemed impossible.

The Story of the Small Garage

Many global companies today began in extremely modest conditions.

Some started in small apartments. Others began in garages or tiny rented rooms.

In the early days, the founders did not possess vast resources or powerful connections. What they possessed was something far more important: a clear vision of what could be built.

That vision guided their decisions. It encouraged them to continue working when progress felt slow.

It helped them overcome skepticism from people who could not yet see the same future.

Over time, consistent effort transformed those early ideas into real businesses.

But without vision, those journeys would never have begun.

Vision Creates Direction

One of the greatest benefits of vision is that it provides direction. When individuals know what they are working toward, their daily actions gain purpose. Small decisions begin aligning with larger goals.

A person who envisions financial independence may begin learning about investing.

Someone who dreams of building a business may start studying markets, customers, and management skills.

Step by step, the vision begins shaping behavior.

Without vision, effort can become scattered. Energy is spent in many directions without producing meaningful progress.

But when a clear goal exists, effort becomes focused and powerful.

Protecting Your Vision

Vision must also be protected. Not everyone will understand your goals. Some people may doubt your ideas or question your ambitions.

This does not necessarily come from negativity. Sometimes people simply project their own limitations onto others.

If someone believes certain achievements are impossible for them, they may assume the same for everyone else.

For this reason, successful individuals learn to guard their vision carefully.

They remain open to advice and learning, but they do not allow doubt from others to extinguish their ambition. Instead, they allow their vision to grow stronger through discipline, learning, and persistence.

Turning Vision Into Action

Vision alone is not enough. Dreams that remain only in the imagination never create results.

Vision becomes powerful when it is combined with action. This means taking the first small steps even when the final destination still feels far away.

- A writer begins by drafting the first chapter.
- An entrepreneur begins by testing a simple idea.
- An investor begins by learning the basic principles of finance.

Each step may appear small, but over time those steps accumulate into meaningful progress.

Vision provides the destination. Action creates the path.

The Silent Rule

The eighth silent rule of wealth can be summarized in a powerful truth:

- People who build extraordinary lives first imagine them.

Vision creates direction, fuels persistence, and transforms ordinary effort into purposeful progress.

Rule #9

Faith And Purpose

At the beginning of the journey, many people pursue wealth for practical reasons.

- They want financial security.
- They want freedom from constant financial stress.
- They want the ability to support their families and live comfortably.

These goals are understandable and important.

But as individuals progress further along the path of wealth creation, many begin to discover something surprising that money alone rarely brings lasting fulfillment.

Wealth can provide comfort, opportunity, and influence. Yet without a deeper purpose, even great financial success can feel incomplete.

This is why the final silent rule of wealth involves something greater than money. It involves faith and purpose.

The Role of Faith

Faith can take many forms. For some, it is spiritual belief. For others, it is a deep trust in their own ability to grow and overcome challenges.

Regardless of its form, faith plays a powerful role in the journey toward success.

There will always be moments of uncertainty. There will be setbacks, failures, and unexpected obstacles. Plans will sometimes fall apart. Opportunities may disappear just when they seemed close.

During these moments, logic alone is not always enough to sustain determination.

Faith becomes the force that keeps people moving forward when results are not yet visible.

It is the quiet belief that effort will eventually lead to progress.

It is the confidence that setbacks are temporary and that new opportunities will appear.

Many of history's most determined individuals relied on this kind of belief to continue pursuing their goals during difficult times.

Discovering Purpose

Beyond faith lies another powerful motivator: purpose.

Purpose answers an important question: "Why am I building wealth?"

For some people, the answer involves family. They want to provide opportunities for their children that they never had.

For others, purpose comes from creating something meaningful—a business that improves lives, a product that solves problems, or ideas that inspire people.

Purpose transforms wealth from a personal goal into something larger, It shifts the focus from accumulation to impact.

When individuals understand the deeper reason behind their ambitions, their work gains new energy. Challenges become easier to face because the mission is greater than personal comfort.

The Silent Rule

The ninth silent rule of wealth can be expressed simply:

- True wealth is not only about what you gain. It is also about what you give and what you leave behind.

Money can create freedom. But purpose gives that freedom meaning.

Faith provides strength during difficult moments. And Purpose ensures that the impact of your work continues far beyond your own limits.

Rule #10

Time Is the Greatest Asset

When most people think about wealth, they think about money. They imagine bank accounts, investments, businesses, and expensive assets. But in reality, the most valuable resource every person possesses is not money. It is time.

Money can be lost and earned again. Businesses can fail and be rebuilt. Opportunities may disappear but later return in new forms.

But time has one unique characteristic. Once it passes, it never comes back.

This simple truth makes time the most powerful and valuable asset anyone can manage.

The Hidden Cost of Wasted Time

Many people underestimate how much time they waste every day. Hours disappear through distractions, unnecessary arguments, endless scrolling on social media, and activities that bring no meaningful progress.

A single wasted hour may seem harmless. But when those hours accumulate over months and years, they become something much more serious.

Lost potential.

Imagine two individuals starting their lives at the same point.

The first spends several hours every day learning new skills, reading books, improving their knowledge, and working toward long-term goals.

The second spends those same hours in entertainment, distractions, and activities that do not build future value.

At first, the difference between them is invisible. But after five years, their lives begin to look very different. After ten years, the gap becomes enormous.

Time, when used wisely, becomes a powerful investment. When wasted, it becomes an opportunity that can never be recovered.

Investing Time Instead of Spending It

Most people understand how to spend money. But very few people learn how to invest their time.

Spending time means using it on activities that bring temporary enjoyment but little long-term benefit. Investing time means using it in ways that create future value.

Examples of time investment include:

- Learning new skills
- Building a business
- Studying financial knowledge
- Improving health and discipline
- Developing relationships with valuable mentors

These activities may not produce immediate rewards. But over time, they create opportunities that would otherwise never exist.

Just like money in an investment account grows through compound interest, time invested wisely creates compound progress.

A Story of Two Evenings

Consider two young professionals who both finish work at 6 PM every evening.

The first spends the rest of the night watching television and browsing the internet until midnight.

The second uses a few of those evening hours to learn about digital marketing and business strategy.

At first, nothing seems different between them. But after one year, the second individual has gained hundreds of hours of valuable knowledge.

After three years, they may have started a small side business. After five years, that side business may have grown into a powerful source of income.

The difference began with something simple: how they used their time each evening.

The Discipline of Priorities

Using time wisely requires discipline. Not every opportunity deserves your attention. Not every activity deserves your energy.

Successful individuals learn to ask an important question: "Is this helping me build the future I want?"

If the answer is no, they reduce the time spent on that activity. Instead, they focus their attention on actions that move their goals forward.

This does not mean eliminating enjoyment from life. Rest, recreation, and relationships are essential for balance. But the difference lies in intentional living. Every hour becomes a choice.

The Silent Rule

The tenth silent rule of wealth is simple but powerful:

- Those who respect time eventually earn the rewards of time.

People who invest their hours wisely build skills, relationships, and opportunities that multiply over the years. People who waste their time often discover too late that opportunities have quietly passed them by.

The journey toward wealth therefore begins with a simple but important realization:

You may not control how much time you have in life. But you can always control how you use the time you are given.

And those who learn to master their time often discover that success begins to follow.

Rule #11

Skills Pay More Than Degrees

While education remains valuable, the modern world has revealed an important truth: Degrees open doors, but skills create wealth.

Many highly educated individuals struggle financially, while others with strong practical skills build powerful businesses and careers.

The difference lies in value creation. Skills are the tools that allow a person to solve problems, create products, build systems, and serve others effectively. The more valuable the skill, the greater the potential reward.

The Marketplace Rewards Value

In the real world, income is often connected to the value a person provides.

- Someone who can sell products effectively increases a company's revenue.

- Someone who understands technology can build systems that improve efficiency.

- Someone who communicates ideas clearly can influence audiences and inspire action.

These abilities are not simply academic knowledge. They are practical skills that produce results i.e. The marketplace rewards results.

This is why individuals who continuously develop useful skills often find themselves surrounded by opportunities.

Learning Never Stops

One of the most powerful habits of successful individuals is continuous learning.

They do not stop learning after formal education ends. Instead, they treat life itself as an ongoing classroom.

They read books, attend seminars, study new technologies, and observe how successful people operate.

Each new skill becomes another tool in their toolbox.

Over time, this growing collection of skills allows them to adapt to changing industries and seize opportunities others may miss.

A Story of Determination

Consider the story of a young man who worked as a cashier in a small electronics store.

The job paid modestly, and many people viewed it as temporary work.

But instead of simply completing his daily tasks, he paid close attention to the products being sold. He studied how customers made purchasing decisions and how certain products attracted more interest.

In his spare time, he began learning about digital marketing.

Within a year, he was helping the store improve its online promotions. Sales increased significantly, and management noticed his contribution. And soon he was promoted.

Later, he used those same marketing skills to start his own online business.

What began as a simple cashier job became the starting point for a new career because he chose to build skills instead of remaining comfortable.

The Power of Transferable Skills

Another advantage of valuable skills is that they often transfer across industries.

For example:

- A person who understands marketing can apply that knowledge to retail, technology, education, or entertainment.

- A skilled negotiator can succeed in business partnerships, sales, or leadership roles.

- A strong communicator can teach, inspire, and lead in many environments.

These abilities travel with the individual, creating opportunities wherever they go.

This flexibility makes skilled individuals highly valuable in a rapidly changing world.

The Silent Rule

The eleventh silent rule of wealth can be summarized in one clear idea:

- The more valuable your skills, the more valuable your time becomes.

Education provides a foundation. But it is the continuous development of practical abilities that often leads to financial growth and independence.

Those who invest in their skills create opportunities that no economic condition can easily remove. And as those skills grow, and something interesting begins to happen.

People begin to notice, opportunities begin to appear, abd success becomes less about luck and more about preparation.

Rule #12

Solve Bigger Problems

One of the simplest ways to understand wealth is through a single principle: The size of your income often reflects the size of the problems you solve.

People who solve small problems usually earn small rewards. People who solve large problems often receive much greater compensation.

This is not a strict rule, but it appears consistently throughout business, entrepreneurship, and innovation.

When someone creates solutions that improve lives, increase efficiency, or save time, others are willing to pay for that value.

The Value of Solutions

Every successful business exists because it solves a problem.

- A transportation company solves the problem of travel.
- A software company solves the problem of efficiency.
- A restaurant solves the problem of hunger and convenience.

When individuals learn to recognize problems around them, they also begin seeing opportunities.

Instead of complaining about challenges, they begin asking:

- How can this problem be solved?
- Is there a better way to do this?
- What improvement could make life easier for others?

These questions often lead to ideas that eventually become businesses or innovations.

A Story of Observation

A young entrepreneur once noticed something frustrating while working in a busy office.

Employees spent large amounts of time organizing files manually. Important documents were frequently misplaced, causing delays and confusion.

Instead of ignoring the problem, he began exploring possible solutions.

He studied simple software tools and eventually created a basic digital system that allowed files to be stored and searched easily.

The improvement saved hours of work each week. Soon other companies became interested in the same solution.

What began as a small attempt to solve a simple office problem eventually turned into a growing technology business.

Thinking Bigger

Many people limit themselves by thinking too small. They focus only on personal income instead of broader value.

But those who learn to think bigger begin looking for challenges that affect many people at once.

For example:

- A teacher improves the education of hundreds of students.

- A medical researcher develops treatments that help thousands of patients.

- An entrepreneur creates a product used by millions.

The larger the impact, the greater the potential value.

The Silent Rule

The twelfth silent rule of wealth can be expressed clearly:

- If you want greater rewards, focus on solving greater problems.

Opportunity often hides inside challenges. Those who train themselves to see solutions where others see obstacles often discover that wealth begins with a simple act of helping others overcome difficulties.

And when individuals continue solving problems consistently, they develop something extremely powerful.

They develop trust and reputation. Which leads us to the next principle.

Rule #13

Reputation Is Currency

In the world of wealth and opportunity, money is not the only form of currency.

There is another asset that quietly influences success in powerful ways. And that asset is reputation.

Reputation is the collection of beliefs people hold about your character, your reliability, and your integrity. It is built slowly through actions, decisions, and the way you treat others.

Unlike money, reputation cannot be printed or borrowed. It must be earned over time. But once established, it becomes one of the most valuable assets a person can possess.

The Trust Advantage

When people trust you, opportunities begin to appear naturally.

Business partners feel confident working with you. Clients are willing to buy from you. Investors feel comfortable placing resources in your hands.

Trust reduces uncertainty. In a world where people constantly evaluate risk, trust becomes a powerful advantage.

A person with a strong reputation often receives opportunities before others even know those opportunities exist.

This is because people prefer working with individuals whose character they respect.

The Fragile Nature of Reputation

While reputation is powerful, it is also fragile. It can take years to build but only moments to damage.

Dishonesty, broken promises, or unethical decisions can quickly erode the trust that took so long to establish.

This is why successful individuals often protect their reputation carefully.

- They keep their word.
- They treat others fairly.
- They accept responsibility for their mistakes.

These habits create a foundation of trust that becomes more valuable over time.

A Story of Integrity

A young entrepreneur once signed a contract to deliver a large order of products to a retailer.

Shortly before the delivery date, unexpected supply problems increased his costs dramatically. If he completed the order at the agreed price, he would lose money.

Many people advised him to cancel the contract or demand a higher price. But he chose a different path.

He honored the agreement and delivered the products exactly as promised, even though it meant accepting a financial loss.

Months later, the retailer offered him a much larger contract, explaining that his honesty had made a strong impression.

What seemed like a short-term loss turned into a long-term opportunity because he protected his reputation.

Reputation in the Digital Age

In today's connected world, reputation travels faster than ever before.

Reviews, recommendations, and online discussions can influence how thousands of people perceive a business or individual.

This means that integrity has become even more important.

- One positive experience can bring new customers and partnerships.
- One negative experience can spread quickly and damage years of work.

For this reason, many successful individuals focus not only on making profits but also on creating positive experiences for others. Satisfied customers, grateful partners, and respected colleagues all contribute to a strong reputation.

The Silent Rule

The thirteenth silent rule of wealth can be summarized in a simple statement:

- A strong reputation opens doors that money alone cannot unlock.

When people trust you, opportunities multiply. Partnerships grow stronger. Businesses expand more easily. And success becomes easier to sustain.

Reputation is therefore not just a moral value—it is also a powerful economic asset.

And as individuals continue building trust and credibility, another important factor begins to shape their success.

The ability to learn faster than the world changes around them.

Rule #14

Learn Faster Than Others

The world is constantly changing.

New technologies appear. Industries evolve. Economic conditions shift. Ideas that once dominated entire markets can suddenly become outdated.

In such an environment, one of the greatest advantages a person can develop is the ability to learn quickly and continuously.

Those who stop learning often find themselves left behind. Those who continue learning remain prepared for the future.

The Speed of Change

In previous generations, industries changed slowly. A skill learned early in life could remain valuable for decades.

Today, knowledge evolves at an incredible pace.

New tools and technologies appear every year. Entire industries can transform within a short period of time.

This means that success is no longer determined only by what you already know. It is also determined by how quickly you can learn what you do not yet know.

The Habit of Curiosity

Successful individuals often share a common habit: curiosity.

- They ask questions.
- They explore unfamiliar topics.
- They remain open to new ideas even when those ideas challenge their existing beliefs.

Curiosity fuels learning. It encourages people to explore possibilities others may overlook.

And over time, this constant exploration leads to deeper knowledge and better decision-making.

A Story of Adaptation

A small bookstore owner once faced a difficult situation.

As digital technology grew, many customers began purchasing books online instead of visiting physical stores. Sales began declining, and the future of the business seemed uncertain.

Instead of resisting change, the owner chose to learn about digital marketing and online sales platforms.

Soon he launched an online store connected to his physical shop. He also began hosting community reading events and book discussions that attracted local readers.

The combination of online convenience and community experience allowed his business to survive and eventually grow.

His willingness to learn something new saved the company.

Learning as an Investment

Just like money invested in assets, knowledge invested in the mind produces long-term returns.

Books, courses, conversations with mentors, and personal experiments all contribute to growth.

Each new idea becomes another tool for solving problems and creating opportunities.

The more tools you possess, the more valuable you become in the marketplace.

The Silent Rule

The fourteenth silent rule of wealth is simple:

- The person who learns the fastest often wins the future.

When industries change, learners adapt. When opportunities appear, learners recognize them. And when challenges arise, learners discover solutions.

In a rapidly evolving world, knowledge is no longer static. It is a moving target.

Those who chase it continuously often find themselves standing at the front of progress.

Rule #15

Control Your Lifestyle Inflation

One of the most common financial traps is something called lifestyle inflation. It happens quietly.

A person receives a raise at work. Suddenly they move to a more expensive apartment. They buy a newer car. They upgrade their phone, clothes, and entertainment.

At first, these upgrades feel like rewards for hard work. But something strange happens.

Even though income increases, financial pressure often remains the same.

Why?

Because expenses increased just as quickly.

This pattern traps many people in a cycle where they earn more money every year but never actually become wealthier.

The Illusion of Progress

Lifestyle inflation creates the illusion of success.

From the outside, it may appear that a person is doing extremely well. They own impressive things and live comfortably.

But behind the scenes, their financial position may not be improving.

- Savings remain low.

- Investments are limited.
- Unexpected emergencies create stress.

The problem is not income. The problem is spending habits.

True wealth grows when income increases while expenses remain controlled.

The Discipline of Balance

Controlling lifestyle inflation does not mean avoiding enjoyment or living in constant restriction.

Life should be enjoyed.

However, financially disciplined individuals follow a different balance.

When their income rises, they increase their investments and savings first, before expanding their lifestyle.

Instead of asking, "What can I buy with this extra money?"

They ask a different question: "How can this money strengthen my future?"

Part of the increase may go toward better living conditions, but a significant portion is directed toward assets that grow over time. This simple habit creates a powerful advantage.

A Story of Two Promotions

Two employees at a company received promotions in the same year. Both saw their salaries increase significantly.

The first employee celebrated by immediately upgrading his lifestyle. He purchased a luxury car, moved into a larger apartment, and began spending more on entertainment.

The second employee made smaller lifestyle improvements but directed most of the extra income toward investments and savings.

Five years later, their situations were very different.

The first employee was still dependent on each paycheck to maintain his lifestyle.

The second employee had built a strong investment portfolio and was steadily approaching financial independence.

Both earned the same promotion. But their financial futures were shaped by different choices.

The Wealth Builder's Rule

Financial progress often depends on a simple principle:

- Increase your assets faster than your lifestyle.
- When assets grow consistently, wealth begins to accumulate.
- When lifestyle grows too quickly, wealth struggles to appear.

This discipline may feel challenging at first, especially when surrounded by a culture that encourages constant spending.

But those who master this habit often discover something remarkable.

They gain freedom.

- Freedom from financial stress.
- Freedom from constant dependence on income.
- And freedom to make choices based on opportunity rather than necessity.

The Silent Rule

The fifteenth silent rule of wealth can be expressed clearly:

- If your lifestyle grows faster than your investments, wealth will always remain out of reach.

- But if your investments grow faster than your lifestyle, financial independence begins to move closer.

Those who understand this difference quietly build strong financial foundations while others remain trapped in endless cycles of spending.

And once a person learns to control their lifestyle, they become ready for another important skill.

The ability to protect their financial resources and avoid unnecessary risks.

Rule #16

Protect Your Capital

Building wealth takes time, effort, and discipline. But losing wealth can happen very quickly.

A single reckless decision, a poorly researched investment, or an impulsive business move can erase years of progress.

For this reason, successful investors and entrepreneurs follow a powerful principle: Protect your capital.

Capital represents the resources used to create future wealth. It may include savings, investments, equipment, property, or business assets.

Without capital, it becomes difficult to seize opportunities. Protecting it therefore becomes a top priority.

The First Rule of Wealth Protection

Many experienced investors follow a simple philosophy:

- Rule one: Never lose money unnecessarily.
- Rule two: Never forget rule one.

This does not mean avoiding all risk. Every investment carries some level of uncertainty.

But wise individuals carefully evaluate risks before committing their resources.

They research opportunities, study market conditions, and consider worst-case scenarios.

If a decision could destroy their financial stability, they approach it with caution.

Avoiding the "All-In" Trap

One of the most dangerous financial habits is placing all resources into a single opportunity.

Sometimes people become excited about a business idea, a stock market tip, or a new investment trend.

Believing they have discovered something special, they commit everything they have.

If the investment succeeds, the reward may be large. But if it fails, the loss can be devastating.

Wealth builders usually avoid this approach. Instead, they spread risk across multiple opportunities. This strategy reduces the chances that one mistake will destroy their entire financial position.

A Story of Patience

An investor once encountered an exciting new startup company. The idea seemed promising, and many people rushed to invest large amounts of money.

Instead of following the crowd, the investor chose patience. He studied the company carefully, examined its financial structure, and waited to see how the business performed during its first year.

During that time, the company began facing serious management problems.

Investors who rushed in early lost significant money. While the patient investor avoided the loss simply by taking time to evaluate the opportunity.

Sometimes the best financial decision is not immediate action, but careful observation.

Long-Term Thinking

Protecting capital also involves thinking long term.

Short-term opportunities may appear attractive, but they sometimes carry hidden risks.

Individuals who focus on sustainable growth often choose investments that can survive economic changes and continue producing value over time.

They prioritize stability and steady progress over quick gains. This mindset protects their financial foundation.

The Silent Rule

The sixteenth silent rule of wealth can be summarized simply:

- It is not enough to grow money. You must also protect it.

Those who preserve their capital remain prepared for future opportunities.

Those who lose their capital often spend years rebuilding what was lost.

And when capital is protected and managed wisely, it becomes possible to do something even more powerful.

It becomes possible to build systems that generate wealth consistently.

Rule #17

Build Systems, Not Just Income

Many people spend their lives chasing income.

They work harder, take extra shifts, or search for higher-paying jobs. Their focus is always on earning more money through their personal effort.

While this approach can improve income, it often has a hidden limitation. **"Time".**

A person can only work a limited number of hours in a day. Even the most hardworking individual eventually reaches a ceiling where income cannot grow further without sacrificing health, family, or personal freedom.

This is where the concept of systems becomes important.

The Difference Between Income and Systems

Income is money earned through direct effort.

For example:

- A salary from a job
- Payment for services
- Wages for hours worked

Systems, however, are structures that continue generating income even when you are not actively working.

Examples of systems include:

- A business that operates with employees or automated processes
- Investments that generate dividends or interest
- Digital products that sell repeatedly
- Rental properties producing monthly income

The key difference is simple.

Income requires constant effort. Systems continue functioning with less direct involvement.

The Power of Multiplication

When people rely only on personal labor, their earning potential grows slowly.

But when they build systems, their financial potential multiplies.

A business owner, for instance, does not rely solely on personal work. Instead, the business operates through a network of employees, suppliers, and customers.

The system produces results beyond the owner's individual capacity.

Similarly, an investor's capital works within financial markets, generating returns without constant supervision.

Systems allow one person's effort to expand far beyond their personal limitations.

A Story of a Small Idea

A young designer once started creating simple digital templates for presentations and business documents.

At first, he sold a few copies online. The income was small, but the idea had an interesting advantage.

Once the template was created, it could be sold repeatedly without needing to be redesigned each time.

Over the next few years, the designer continued adding new templates to his online store.

Gradually, the small collection grew into a large library of products.

Thousands of customers purchased the templates across different countries.

The designer was no longer selling only his time. He had created a system that continued producing income.

Designing Your Own System

Not every system must be large or complex. Some begin with small ideas that gradually expand.

A person may start a small business selling products locally, then build a distribution network.

Another may invest in assets that slowly generate passive income. Others may create content, books, or digital resources that reach audiences around the world.

The important factor is not the size of the system at the beginning. It is the direction of growth.

Systems create the possibility of income that expands beyond personal effort.

The Silent Rule

The seventeenth silent rule of wealth can be expressed clearly:

- Do not only work for money. Build systems that allow money to work for you.

Those who rely solely on labor may remain trapped within the limits of time.

Those who build systems gradually unlock the ability to grow beyond those limits.

And as systems grow, another challenge appears. Managing the most limited resource of all.

"Time".

Rule #18

Master Your Time

Time is the one resource that every person receives equally. Every day contains twenty-four hours.

No one can buy extra hours or store unused time for later.

Yet despite this equality, some individuals accomplish extraordinary things while others struggle to make progress. The difference often lies in how time is used.

The Hidden Cost of Distraction

Modern life offers endless distractions. Social media, entertainment, constant notifications, and countless other activities compete for attention.

While these things may provide relaxation or enjoyment, they can quietly consume hours without producing meaningful progress.

A person may feel busy all day yet accomplish very little. Over time, these small distractions accumulate into significant lost opportunities.

Successful individuals often develop the ability to recognize and control distractions. They choose carefully where their time is invested.

The Value of Focus

Focus is the ability to direct attention toward a single meaningful task without interruption.

When people work with deep concentration, they produce better results in less time.

A project that might normally take several days can sometimes be completed in a few focused hours.

This is why many high achievers schedule periods of uninterrupted work.

During these moments, they eliminate distractions and concentrate entirely on important tasks. And the results are often remarkable.

A Story of Priorities

A young entrepreneur once complained that he never had enough time to work on his business ideas.

His mentor asked him a simple question. "Show me how you spend your day."

After reviewing his daily schedule, the mentor noticed several hours spent scrolling through social media, watching random videos, and engaging in unproductive conversations.

The mentor smiled and said, "You do not lack time. You lack priorities."

The entrepreneur gradually replaced some of those habits with focused work. And within a year, his small business began generating steady income.

The time had always been available. It simply needed to be used differently.

Time and Wealth

Money lost can sometimes be recovered. Opportunities missed may appear again in new forms. But time lost is permanent.

This is why many successful individuals treat time with extraordinary respect.

They plan their days carefully. They eliminate activities that provide little value. And they dedicate their best hours to meaningful work.

The Silent Rule

The eighteenth silent rule of wealth is simple yet powerful:

- Where your time goes, your future follows.

Time invested in growth produces progress. Time wasted on distractions produces regret.

Those who learn to direct their time wisely often discover that productivity, success, and opportunity begin to increase rapidly.

And once time is mastered, the next challenge emerges. The ability to develop a mindset strong enough to face failure without surrender.

Rule #19

Learn From Failure Without Fear

Failure is often misunderstood.

Many people see it as proof that they are not capable, not intelligent enough, or not prepared for success. Because of this belief, they avoid risks and opportunities that might lead to failure.

But in reality, failure is one of the most powerful teachers in the journey toward success.

Almost every successful individual has experienced setbacks, mistakes, and moments of disappointment.

What separates them from others is not the absence of failure. It is their response to it.

The Fear That Stops Progress

Fear of failure can quietly limit a person's potential.

- Someone with a business idea may hesitate to start because they worry about losing money.

- An aspiring writer may avoid sharing their work because they fear criticism.

- An entrepreneur may delay launching a product because they worry it will not succeed.

In each case, the fear of failure prevents progress before the journey even begins.

But avoiding failure often means avoiding opportunity as well. Growth rarely happens within the comfort of certainty.

The Hidden Value of Mistakes

Every mistake contains information.

- A failed investment reveals what not to do next time.
- A business challenge teaches lessons about markets, customers, and strategy.
- A rejected proposal may highlight areas for improvement.

These lessons cannot always be learned through theory alone. They are often discovered through experience.

Failure, when approached with the right mindset, becomes a form of education. It reveals weaknesses, strengthens resilience, and sharpens judgment.

A Story of Persistence

A young inventor once created a new product he believed would transform his industry.

Excited by the idea, he invested his savings and launched the product into the market.

Unfortunately, the launch was a failure. Customers showed little interest, and the product quickly disappeared from stores.

Many people would have abandoned the idea of entrepreneurship entirely. Instead, the inventor studied what went wrong.

He discovered that his product solved a real problem, but the design was complicated and difficult for customers to use.

Using this knowledge, he redesigned the product and launched a new version. This time, the product succeeded and eventually became widely adopted.

The first failure was not the end of the journey. It was simply a step in the learning process.

Resilience and Growth

Failure also builds resilience.

Resilience is the ability to continue moving forward despite obstacles or disappointment.

When people experience challenges and overcome them, their confidence grows.

They learn that setbacks are temporary and that persistence often leads to improvement.

Over time, resilience becomes a powerful advantage. While others abandon their goals after difficulties, resilient individuals continue progressing.

The Silent Rule

The nineteenth silent rule of wealth can be summarized simply:

- Failure is not the opposite of success, it is part of the path toward it.

Those who fear failure often remain stuck in hesitation. Those who learn from failure gain knowledge, strength, and experience.

And as individuals develop resilience, they begin to understand an even deeper truth.

Success is rarely achieved alone. It often grows through collaboration, partnerships, and meaningful relationships.

Rule #20

The Power of Relationships

No great success story is built in complete isolation.

Behind most achievements, there are relationships—mentors who offered guidance, partners who shared responsibilities, and communities that provided support.

Human connection plays a powerful role in the journey toward success.

Opportunity Through Connection

Many opportunities appear through relationships rather than formal applications.

- A business partner may introduce a new opportunity.
- A mentor may share valuable knowledge.
- A friend may recommend someone for a position or project.

These connections create networks through which information, opportunities, and resources flow.

The stronger and more genuine these relationships are, the more powerful the network becomes.

The Principle of Mutual Value

Strong relationships are rarely built on one-sided benefit. They grow when both individuals contribute value to each other.

This value may come in many forms:

- Knowledge and advice
- Business collaboration
- Emotional support
- Shared opportunities

When people consistently help others succeed, they often discover that support returns in unexpected ways.

Relationships built on trust and generosity tend to last much longer than those built on short-term advantage.

A Story of a Mentor

A young professional once approached a successful entrepreneur and asked for advice.

Instead of asking for money or investment, he simply asked questions and listened carefully to the responses.

Over time, the young professional applied the lessons he received and continued updating the entrepreneur about his progress.

The entrepreneur noticed the young man's dedication and willingness to learn.

Eventually, he invited him to join a new business project. That opportunity became the turning point in the young man's career.

The relationship began not with a request for success, but with respect and curiosity.

Reputation and Relationships

Relationships are closely connected to reputation.

People prefer working with individuals they trust, respect, and enjoy being around.

This is why qualities such as honesty, reliability, and kindness often play a significant role in professional success.

A person may possess excellent technical skills, but if others find them difficult to work with, opportunities may disappear.

On the other hand, individuals who build positive relationships often discover doors opening throughout their careers.

The Silent Rule

The twentieth silent rule of wealth is clear:

- Your network often determines the opportunities you encounter.

Strong relationships expand knowledge, create partnerships, and open pathways that may otherwise remain hidden.

When people invest time and energy into building genuine connections, they create an environment where success becomes more likely.

Rule #21

Define Your Purpose

Money can buy comfort. It can provide security, opportunities, and freedom from many of life's financial worries. Yet history shows that wealth alone does not always create fulfillment.

Many individuals achieve financial success but later find themselves asking an important question: "What is all of this for?"

This question leads to the idea of purpose.

Purpose is the deeper reason behind the pursuit of success. It gives direction to effort and meaning to achievement.

- Without purpose, wealth can feel empty.
- With purpose, wealth becomes a powerful tool for impact.

The Difference Between Goals and Purpose

Goals and purpose are related, but they are not the same.

A goal is something specific you want to achieve, such as building a successful company, publishing a book, or reaching financial independence.

Purpose is the larger reason behind those goals.

For example:

- A person may build a business not only to earn money, but to create jobs and improve communities.

- A writer may publish books not only for success, but to inspire and educate readers.

- An entrepreneur may pursue wealth in order to support family and future generations.

Purpose transforms goals into something meaningful.

A Story of Legacy

A successful business owner once spent decades building a large company. Through discipline and persistence, he accumulated significant wealth.

As he grew older, he began reflecting on the impact of his work. He realized that the most meaningful moments of his career were not the profits or the deals he had closed.

They were the lives that had changed because of the company.

- Employees who built careers.
- Families supported through stable jobs.
- Communities strengthened through economic growth.

He understood that the business had become more than a financial success. It had become part of his legacy.

Purpose Creates Motivation

When people connect their work to a meaningful purpose, their motivation becomes stronger.

- Difficult challenges feel more manageable.
- Long hours feel worthwhile.
- Temporary failures become easier to overcome.

Purpose acts like a compass that guides decisions and keeps individuals moving forward even when progress feels slow. It transforms effort into something larger than personal gain.

Discovering Your Purpose

Purpose is not always discovered instantly.

For many people, it emerges gradually through experience, reflection, and personal growth.

Some find purpose in creating solutions to problems. Others find it in helping people grow, building communities, or sharing knowledge.

The important thing is not that purpose must be grand or dramatic. It simply needs to be meaningful to the person pursuing it.

The Silent Rule

The twenty-first silent rule of wealth can be summarized in a simple idea:

- Money is powerful, but purpose gives money meaning.

When wealth is guided by purpose, success becomes more fulfilling and lasting.

It creates impact that extends beyond personal benefit. And when individuals begin thinking about purpose, they naturally begin thinking about something even larger. **"Legacy".** The lasting influence they leave behind.

Rule #22

Build a Legacy

Success is often measured by achievements during one lifetime. But legacy asks a deeper question: "What will remain after you are gone?"

Legacy is the long-term influence created by a person's actions, values, and contributions. It is not limited to wealth alone.

Legacy can be found in ideas, businesses, books, communities, and the lives of people who were inspired along the way.

The Ripple Effect

Every action has the potential to influence others.

- A teacher may inspire students who later become leaders.

- An entrepreneur may build a company that continues serving people for decades.

- A writer may publish ideas that shape the thinking of future generations.

These contributions create a ripple effect that extends far beyond a single moment.

Legacy grows through these ripples of influence.

Financial Legacy

One part of legacy involves financial resources.

Wealth can support families, fund education, build institutions, and create opportunities for future generations.

Many successful individuals therefore think carefully about how their resources will be used in the future.

They plan investments, charitable contributions, and long-term projects that will continue making a positive difference.

In this way, wealth becomes a tool for lasting impact.

A Story of Generational Thinking

A farmer once planted a row of large trees along the edge of his land.

A neighbor asked why he was planting trees that would take many years to grow fully.

The farmer smiled and replied, "Because someone planted trees before I was born, and I have enjoyed their shade my entire life."

His actions were not only for his own benefit. They were for the people who would come after him.

This is the essence of legacy thinking.

Living With Legacy in Mind

When people think about legacy, their decisions often change.

- Short-term gains become less important than long-term impact.
- Integrity becomes more valuable than temporary advantage.

And the focus shifts from personal success to contributions that benefit others.

Legacy encourages individuals to build things that last.

The Silent Rule

The twenty-second silent rule of wealth is simple but profound:

- True success is measured not only by what you gain, but by what you leave behind.

When individuals think about legacy, their work becomes larger than themselves.

Their ideas, efforts, and contributions begin shaping the future in ways they may never fully see.

And with this final principle, the journey through the silent rules of wealth reaches its conclusion.

Conclusion

The Silent Path to Success

Success rarely appears overnight.

Behind every meaningful achievement lies a series of quiet principles practiced consistently over time.

Throughout this journey, we have explored the silent rules that guide individuals toward lasting prosperity:

- Understanding the power of discipline
- Investing in knowledge and growth
- Building systems rather than relying only on effort
- Protecting capital and managing time wisely
- Learning from failure and building strong relationships
- Discovering purpose and creating a legacy

None of these ideas promise instant results. Instead, they represent a path of steady progress.

A path where small, consistent actions gradually transform into remarkable outcomes.

The silent rules of wealth are not secrets reserved for a select few. They are principles available to anyone willing to apply them with patience and persistence.

And for those who follow this path, success becomes more than financial gain.

It becomes a journey of growth, contribution, and lasting impact.

About the Author

Allan Mirembe is a Ugandan-born, USA bestselling author and award-winning nonfiction writer, best known for his inspiring memoir The Genius Deaf and his captivating dark romance Twisted King. Born on March 26, 2006, Allan lost his hearing in 2014, but turned that challenge into a source of strength and creativity. Through his writing, he blends raw emotion, compelling storytelling, and themes of resilience, love, and self-discovery. He is also the founder of Allan Inspirations, a platform dedicated to empowering young writers and dreamers worldwide. Whether crafting heart-pounding romance or uplifting nonfiction, Allan's mission remains the same to inspire, entertain, and remind readers that even in darkness, light can be found.

www.ingramcontent.com/pod-product-compliance
Lightning Source LLC
LaVergne TN
LVHW022304200926
848481LV00004B/1206
9798295699740